What Does It Mean to Be A

Christian

Written and illustrated by Jeff Todd

Introduction

The guidelines for Christian living have already been written. You can find everything you need to know right there in God's Holy Word - The Bible. It's just a matter of opening it up and reading it. The Spirit of God will reveal to you the things you need to know and give you the ability to understand them.

The purpose of this book is not to be a substitute for reading the Bible. Oh no! Everyone should read it. My hope and intentions for writing this book is that it will inspire you, as the reader, and will offer humorous illustrations to use in your walk with Christ and to put Christianity out there in an easy to understand format. Together we can learn to live our life to the fullest with happiness and joy that God intended for us to live.

First of all, being a Christian doesn't have to be boring and dull. I believe it should be energetic and alive. We are to be a light in the world that we live in and shine out to others. When a person sees the way we are, it should make them want to be that way, too.

Our lifestyle should point them to Jesus. Everything we say and do should reflect the One that saved us.

AFRAID TO SMILE

I have never considered myself to be like everyone else. The way I look at life may be different than the way others see it. Even as a young child, Christian people to me were always the suit and tie-wearing folks or the snooty ladies wearing the dresses and they acted very *'stiff necked'*. It was almost like they were afraid to smile.

I agree, it was wrong of me to segregate Christians like this, but those were the Christians I knew. As I grew older, I realized that not all Christians were like this and were actually normal people.

Being called into the ministry, I have to use what the Lord has given me. This includes the relationship I have with Jesus through His grace that saved me, His Word, and the gifts, talents, and characteristics that He gave me.

When you put that all together in a mixing bowl, you have:

I know from experience that being a Christian isn't a difficult task. It's not a series of rituals or following a magic formula. It's actually so simple that anyone could do it.

That's my purpose and focus of writing this book! I want to write something that would minister to people (no matter who they were) and possibly help them understand what being a Christian is all about.

It's got to be simple and easy to understand. I don't use BIG words when I speak, so why should I write BIG words when I am using this to reach people and lead them to Jesus. I can't! It's not how God made me!

If you're reading this today, this book is for you from a simple minded person like me. Being a Christian is awesome and it's not as weird as you may have heard. We're not crazy people! If you have never asked Jesus to come into your life, I hope and pray that you make that choice today.

If you're already a Christian, I hope this book ministers to you, too. Living the life you profess isn't as hard as you make it when you realize what it's all about. Actually it's not supposed to be hard at all. You're a Christian because you gave your life to Him. Sometimes we have to give it back to Him and let Him lead the way.

Excuse me for a moment. I'll be right back. I need to pray!

Dear Lord, I pray right now that You use these words from this book to reach people out there. I don't know who this is intended for or who will be reading this. I know that I belong to You and that You will use me for your glory. Please do so today. Thank you Jesus. Amen.

So, here it is folks!

What Does It Mean To Be A

Christian

The Starting Point: Jesus

Christian living begins with having Jesus Christ in your life. Period.

Let me say that again because it's important.

Christian living begins with having Jesus Christ in your life. This means that before you can live the life of a Christian, you have to have Jesus as your Lord and Savior in your life. He has to be the center of your life; the foundation that your life sits on. You can't live a Christian life if you're not a Christian.

No *'buts'* about it!

But, I Go To Church

Going to church does not make you a Christian. It makes you a 'church-goer'. Even though you attend church every Sunday, in the morning and at night, it doesn't make you a Christian. You may be a Sunday school teacher and teach from the Bible. It doesn't make you a Christian.

It's almost like calling yourself a fisherman without a fishing pole. Yes, you may go to the lake, but without a pole, you're just a… person that goes to the lake. You may know everything there is to know about fishing. You may know the different types of fish by the color of their fins and the number of sparkles in their eyes, but it doesn't make you a fisherman. You may have the best fishing boat on the lake, but without the pole, you are basically a boat owner. Are you with me?

But, I Have Christian Family

Just because one of your family members is a Christian doesn't make you one. I know this will be hard for people to believe, but being a Christian is not a genetic thing. It's a Jesus thing!

"My grandfather was a deacon at Flakey Biscuit Baptist Church. He was a Christian man that loved the Lord."

That's great! But, it doesn't make you one. The glitter from your Christian relative's walk doesn't magically fall off on you. It would be nice if it did, but it doesn't. Being a Christian and being saved is about a one on one relationship with Jesus Christ.

But, I Shook The Preacher's Hand Last Sunday

If *'hand shaking'* guaranteed a Christian life, then everybody that visited a church on a Sunday morning would be saved and so would every person that the preacher had come in contact with outside of the church. Think about it! Hand shaking is a greeting, not a magic salvation ticket! That's not how it works!

The Deal?

Here's the deal! A person can only become a Christian when they accept Jesus into their life and get saved. Saved? That's right! The day you realize that you are a sinner and that you are lost without a Savior is the day you have a choice of whether to be a Christian or not. The sad thing is that we are all sinners!

For all have sinned, and come short of the glory of God - Romans 3:23

It's like a day at the lake. You jump in and realize you can't swim! Life was pretty smooth when you were playing close to the bank. But as you drifted out towards the deep part of the water, you realize that you needed a float. The same is true in life. You need to be saved or you will sink like a rock!

"That sounds all fine and dandy, but what am I being saved from?"

The answer is sin. It's those *'bad things'* in your life that goes against God and His way of life. To realize how bad sin is, you must first know who God is.

Who Is God?

God created everything. There is nothing in this world, on Earth, or in outer space that He did not create. He created the water, the air, the trees, animals, and He even created you.

The Bible tells us that He knew us before we were even born and that He knew ALL about us. That tells me He's the one that put us here. He put you here!

Before I formed thee in the belly I knew thee; and before thou camest forth out of the womb I sanctified thee, and I ordained thee a prophet unto the nations. – Jeremiah 1: 5

I believe that we are all here for a purpose - His purpose. But, we will never know this purpose until we give our lives to Him. For a God that created everything in this universe to take the time to make me, tells me I have a purpose for being here. The same is true for you! We need to find out what it is. This will involve getting to know the Creator.

Have you heard this one before?:

For whom he did foreknow, he also did predestinate to be conformed to the image of his Son, that he might be the firstborn among many brethren. – Romans 8: 29

He wants a relationship with you. Since you are here and have a purpose, you will need to get a relationship started with God. You will need to know more about Him. The Bible says God is holy and perfect - sinless. Now keep that thought in your mind for a moment and let's talk again about sin.

When you think of the sin in the world today, what comes to mind? Does murder and stealing? What about lying and foul language? There are all kinds of sin! Small ones to big ones and they all have one thing in common - they are still *'sin'*. Sin is what separates us from a relationship with God. We live in a sinful world and

we have sin in our lives. How can we make things right? The unfortunate thing is that WE can't! We need something or someone to fill in that gap. God knew this, too. So what needs to happen?

Don't worry! God already had that planned out because He loves us.

Here's what God did for us! He sent His only Son to die as a sacrifice for our sins. It sounds like a drastic measure to take but it's what was needed. Jesus, His Son, died for us so that we could live - eternally with God.

But wait! His death required something from us?

That's right! It says we have to BELIEVE in Him. Here's another scripture you may have heard:

That if thou shalt confess with thy mouth the Lord Jesus, and shalt believe in thine heart that God hath raised him from the dead, thou shalt be saved. - Romans 10:9

It sounds to me like God has provided a way out for us, but He also requires us to do something to be saved. We already know we are a bunch of sinners. Right?

We are to confess with our mouth the Lord Jesus? And believe in our heart?

Sounds too simple to be true, doesn't it?

It is and it starts with a simple prayer to God. After that, all we have to do is receive this gift of salvation. I believe God convicts our hearts that we are lost. It's like a helpless feeling you have inside that let's you know that you need Him in your life.

Are you feeling that right now? If so, let's get this thing settled. I know a lot of religious people and some Christians get 'weirded out' when you present a model prayer to the lost and ask them to repeat it. I can understand their way of thinking and I know that just repeating prayers doesn't save a person. It has to be heartfelt and sincere. The main points of your prayer has to cover knowing that you're lost without Jesus in your life, understanding that you're a sinner that's sorry for the junk you're doing, and that you are willing to turn from that junk and want Jesus to come in and take over.

That's basically it!

So, if you meet that criteria and would like to accept Jesus as your Lord and Savior, let's do this thing together.

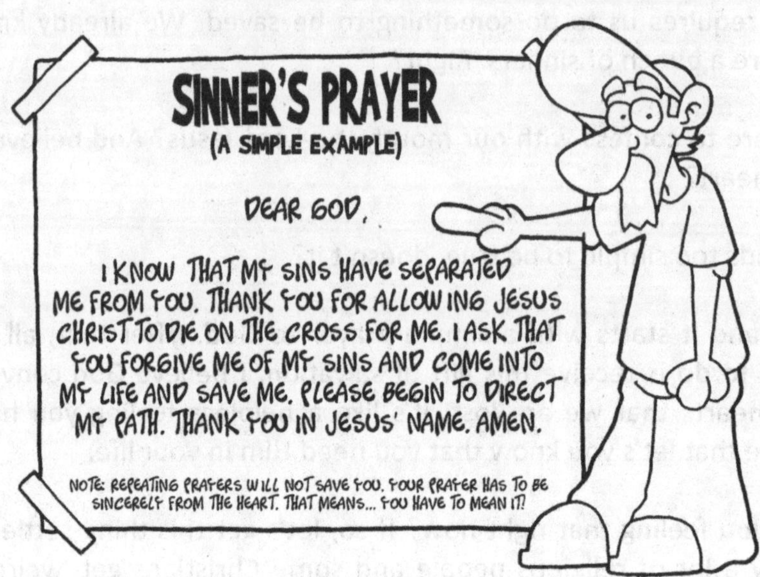

That was easy, wasn't it? Now, I know sparks aren't flying around you and choirs of angels aren't floating by with harps. But, inside you will feel a sense of relief.

It will feel like a ton of bricks have been lifted off your shoulders. Your life may not even show changes immediately, but from this point forward it will. It's like being a new little plant. You will begin growing. That's why they call it being 'born again'. You have a new life! It's up to you make it grow. You can do this by going to church, reading the Bible, and praying every day. Every step in your life from this day on is a 'stepping stone' towards Jesus and growth in your spirituality.

Spiritual Fertilizer

"I'm saved and I know where I'm going when I die. I'm cool with that! But, what should I be doing until then?"

The answer is simple! I should be growing! You should be growing, too! The day we got saved started a new life in us. This is very similar to growing turnip greens in a garden. This new life started as a small seed planted in the ground. Even as a small seed, it's still a turnip green! But you know as well as I do that a plate full of seeds doesn't taste the same as a big plate of turnip greens. The seeds need to grow first.

To help a turnip green grow, it needs some food. Right? It needs some good soil, refreshing water, and some sunlight. The same is true in our Christian walk. Yes, we could stay content with being a seed. But, wouldn't it be better if we started sprouting? A Christian needs some spiritual fertilizer - some food for the soul.

God provides us with ways to grow. All we have to do is use what He gives us. The soil He provides us is through the relationship we can have in Him through prayer and walking with Him daily. Every day is an opportunity.

We just need to take advantage of it.

Finding a Bible-believing church and actually going to it is a great starting point for growth. I will be the first to admit that going to church was not in my plans. As a young saved *'whooper-snapper'*, I wasn't really a *'people'* person and I hated getting up early on a Sunday morning to hear a long-winded preacher spitting and slobbering on the whole congregation.

The music in church was awful and would always come from people that really shouldn't have been up front singing to people anyway. I spent my time in the back row socializing with my friends. I was young and didn't know what the whole *'church thing'* was about and what it was for.

Church: The Growth Experience

Now that I am older, I realize that it was for my spiritual growth as a baby Christian.

This process of getting up on a Sunday morning, getting dressed, and going to a building and hanging out with all of these *'weird'* people was intended to help me grow. My job was to listen and learn.

I also realize that my attitude towards it was wrong and sitting on the back row was my first mistake. For a young teenager like me, I should have been on the front row listening. Now that I look back, maybe my life wouldn't have drifted away from God as it did. I'll explain more on this later on in this book.

What is *'going to church'* all about?

A church building is a place where believers gather to worship and praise God. It's just a building and as I explained earlier, by *'just going'* doesn't save you. Only God can do that! We go there to worship Him and praise

Him for who He is – He's God!

It's also a place to *'get your learning on'*. This is accomplished by singing praises, praying, and listening to what the preacher has to say. God uses these tools to teach us stuff from His Word.

O come, let us sing unto the LORD: let us make a joyful noise to the rock of our salvation. – Psalm 95: 1

Depending on the church, the music is a big part of worship. There are many scriptures throughout the Bible that encourages us to sing songs of praises to God. Actually, the Book of Psalms is simply a book full of song lyrics. It can be in a traditional music style or contemporary music style. It really doesn't matter as long as it's joyful. People will argue about the type of music being played at church and say that only one style is acceptable, but it's not about the style as it is the *'heart'* in which it's worshiped. No one ever taught me this concept about Christian music, but it was in the Bible if I had just taken the time to read it. Plus, when you are singing with right heart, the bad singers start to sound pretty good. Our focus is more on what they are singing instead of how well they sing it. And that's the truth!

A preacher plays a big part in the service because he is a God-called man to deliver the Word. He is the guy that stands in the front of the church with the suit on. If you are in a Baptist church, you will recognize him because he will be the one that speaks the loudest and has the biggest belly. He will be the sweaty man that spits on the congregation sitting on the front row during the services. He is also the first one in line at the *'all you can eat'* buffet dinner restaurant after the church services are over. I'm sorry. I had to throw that in there.

Being a preacher is a big responsibility. The Lord gives him a message to share with the people at church. It is up to him to deliver it. If he delivers something that was not given to him by God, he is going to be in some serious trouble. The preacher has to be very careful in his preaching. He is responsible for what comes out of his mouth.

On the flip side of this, we have to realize that the preacher is just a man. He will make mistakes and is not perfect. Many people will stop going to a particular church or to church, in general, because of something a preacher did that was not acceptable. We should not be followers of preachers, but followers of Jesus Christ. However, we should listen as the Word is being presented to us and follow along with our Bibles open. Listening was another mistake I made earlier in my life.

Preachers ain't perfect! They're human just like we are!

Prayer: For More Growth

Praying is our way of communicating with God. Just like with all types of relationships, good communication is the way to make it stronger. That's why a lot of marriages don't work out. Many times it's because one person does all the talking, or no one is listening, or that nobody talks or listens

at all. It just doesn't work!

Prayer keeps our spiritual life alive! Don't you want to live? Get your prayer on!

By praying to God, we can ask for forgiveness of our sins. We can tell Him how our day is going and let Him know the areas we need help. We can ask for things in our life and even pray for other people's needs. It's like talking to a good friend or better yet, we are talking directly to our Father in Heaven. It helps us to grow spiritually, especially when we see the things we pray for come to pass.

Praying is done in church. It can be done as a group or you can pray as an individual at the altar or right where you sit. But, it's not the only place! You can pray anytime and anywhere. You can pray at home, at somebody else's home, or even on aisle 3 at your local Wally World. It doesn't matter as long as you pray! Most importantly, pray daily!

Bible: The Growth Continues

There's a book that sits around in many homes all over the world.

It's usually the one that's tucked away with dust covering it. It's called the Bible. Even though many people own it, it's rare that people actually read it! For a Christian, it's like an instruction manual for living. It's food for the soul. Its God's words in book form so that we can grow spiritually.

The problem is that many people see it is as just a book with words; like a hard to read novel. It's full of *'thee's'* and *'thou's'* and it's hard to understand. It has stories in there that really don't apply to us, right? Wrong!

Living the Christian life requires reading the instruction manual.

Have you ever tried to put something together or use something without the manual? There were always parts left over or it didn't work the way it's supposed to. Right?

The same is true in our Christian walk. If you try it without the manual, you'll end up face down in the middle of the road. I know from experience, but I am thankful that Jesus was there to pick me up!

There is so much stuff written in the pages of the Bible. It covers everything! Any topic you want to know about, it's in there! There's anything from basic life principles to the history of man. It does include stories of people and their experiences. Why? The purpose is so that we can use their life of accomplishments or mistakes to help make ours better. We can learn from them. It's so cool! The more you put into it, the more you will get out of it.

To sum it all up, basic spiritual growth begins with going to church, prayer and reading the Bible. You can only grow from here!

The Battle Is On! Like A Chicken Bone

Just when you thought that being a Christian was easy, bad things come into your life. Troubles seem to come at you like darts flying at you from everywhere. It may seem like you are now being tempted with things from your past. You may be tempted with things that affect your weaknesses. It's all part of the plan.

It's a battle and we have an enemy! Satan is his name. You may have heard of him. Don't be *'skeered'*! He's not that cute little cartoon you see on television and he's not that scary demon you see in the horror movies. According to the Bible, he is an angel – a fallen angel. He was with God before the world began. He has been trying to mess things up from the day that God created Adam and Eve.

Remember hearing about Adam and Eve?

In the first few chapters of Genesis, you'll read where Satan tempted them into eating the forbidden fruit. By doing so, sin began and it has been growing ever since. He is in the world today along with his band of devils trying to trip people up. He tries to prevent people from getting saved and makes life hard for the average Christian. The purpose in all of this is to mess up God's work in this world and in His work in the people that live in it.

Keep this in mind, God is creating and preparing a place for His people. Folks, this world that we currently live in is not our home! He is returning one day to take his people to their real home. Who gets to go? It's the people that have been saved. That is why Satan works so hard. His days are numbered and he already knows where he's going and it's not good. His purpose is to take people with him - the lost and unsaved. Did you get that?

I bet you're thinking...

I'm saved, so why is he messing with me?

That's an easy question to answer. You could be the link to someone else getting saved. Your witness and testimony could be what leads them to a relationship with the Lord. You will notice that he works on you the hardest when you are trying to live right. If you are living sinfully, Satan doesn't have to do much to you. You have already lost your witnessing ability. What else does he need to do? He's got you right where he wants you - **DEFEATED**.

But, as you grow in the Lord, you are gaining strength and will be used to reach others. Satan hates this idea and will start throwing the darts. He wants you dead and out of the picture! You have become a hindrance to his master minded plans. Watch out!

That's why it is so important to apply the *'spiritual fertilizer'* to your life - church, prayer, and Bible.

When you are following Jesus, you will be able to recognize Satan's devilish schemes against you.

There hath no temptation taken you but such as is common to man: but God is faithful, who will not suffer you to be tempted above that ye are able; but will with the temptation also make a way to escape, that ye may be able to bear it. — 1 Corinthians 10: 13

Here's where it gets tricky. As a child of God, He is watching over you. There is nothing that Satan does to you that God doesn't know about. As mean as it may sound, God allows Satan to tempt you. Yep! That's right! We can learn this from the Book of Job. This doesn't make God bad! It is part of His way of strengthening you as a Christian.

However, He will never let you be tempted more than you can bear without His help!

Temptations are coming. What are they? These will be the things that come into your life that make you think,

"Hmm...Should I or shouldn't I?"

This could be almost anything. Temptations come from Satan and are directed by God. As we discussed earlier, temptations will either make us stronger or they will defeat us if we agree to give in to them.

You can almost know what your temptations will be by knowing what your weaknesses are. If the Lord rescued you from abusing drugs and alcohol, you can be guaranteed that these will come back into your life in the form of a temptation. The temptation in itself is not wrong, it's when you give into them that it becomes a sin. Are you hearing me?

Many people suffer from spiritual depression because they don't know why they are being tempted with these things that may have destroyed them in the past. They think it's their fault and feel like they have been defeated. Here's your wake up call! It's just a

temptation! That's all! Rebuke it and send it back to Satan from where it came! Keep moving on and get over it! Don't let it get you down! If you're down and out because of it, then Satan has won the battle anyway.

Submit yourselves therefore to God. Resist the devil, and he will flee from you. – James 4: 7

Once again, temptations come from Satan. Always remember that! It's important to know.

Trials, on the other hand, are a different story. What are trials? I'll try to explain. Trials, sometimes called 'valleys', enter our lives from time to time. They usually appear when things seem to be going great.

They can almost be like a messed up deer hunting trip. You deer hunters will be able to relate to this. You are wearing your camouflage sitting up in a deer stand. Everything is going great! You have your gun ready and deer are everywhere! It's going to be a great hunting day! All of a sudden it starts to rain! The deer scatter and you have to climb down from the tree soaking wet. Your legs start chaffing as you walk the long trail back to our 4 x 4 pick up truck. You are feeling miserable and you weren't able to get a deer.

Why did this have to happen? Why do you have to go through this?

You call your friend, Bob, on your outdated cell phone telling him what you just went through as you drive back home disgusted with the way the day ended. You are going through all kinds of emotions. You are mad, sad and everything else other than glad. You know what I'm saying?

The next day, you try hunting again. Before you leave, you check the weather report on the news to see if it will rain. The weatherman says, *"It will be sunny all day!"* You bring an umbrella and an extra pair of socks anyway – just in case. This time you pull your trailer carrying your ATV (All Terrain Vehicle) that you got for Christmas last year with you in case of an emergency. Now you are prepared and learned a lesson!

The purpose of this long drawn out story is to say that God is ultimately in control and allows trials to happen in your life to make you stronger. There is something about them that help you develop character. They make you better prepared for future trials and you are able to use the experience to teach others and help them.

Remember Bob from the story? Guess what? He doesn't go deer hunting anymore without bringing an extra pair of socks because he learned something from your experience, too. Pretty cool, huh?

Just like temptations, trials seem to focus on your weak areas in your walk with Jesus.

Suppose you have a love for money and material things. Guess what your trial will be? Yep, you guessed it! Money issues! It could happen in the form of losing your job or down time in your business. Who knows? But, the important things you will learn from it are to trust God with all of your heart, He is your provider – NOT YOU, and to be content with what you have. I know this one from personal experience.

What if you have anger issues? Guess what your trial will be? You will be hit with things in order to make you mad. You will eventually learn to control your temper and thank God for working with you.

The victories come when we *'pass the tests'*. When you are tempted and you are able to push it away, you have just won a victory. Congratulations!

When you are in a trial and you make it through praising God, you have just won a victory. You are on a roll! Now take a look at yourself. You are stronger, better, and more usable to God to win others to Him. It's all part of the process and you're in it! Why would God go through all of this trouble for you?

That's an easy one. He loves you!

The final victory comes when Jesus returns to take us home to be with Him. What an awesome day that will be! Now that you know the basics of being a Christian and what it's all about, it's time to *'walk the walk'*. This means *'being a light in the world'* and sharing what you know about Jesus. I would be lying to you if I said it was easy. It's not! The temptations and the fact that we are all just too lazy prevent

us from doing everything the Lord requires us to do.

Walkin' the Walk

There are a lot of people out there that will say that they are a Christian. It's not up to us to decide if they are speaking the truth. This is up to them and their relationship with God. But, I believe if we are going to say we are a Christian, we need to show it in the way we live our lives. We need to *'walk the walk'*.

As a child of God, our life should show a change. That means we shouldn't be doing the old sinful things we used to do. This life should reflect Jesus. Have you heard the old saying, *"What would Jesus do?"*? This question could be applied to every choice we have to make.

I also know that we aren't perfect. We are going to

make mistakes. But, we shouldn't let that way of thinking prevent us from trying. We should strive to be like Jesus every day.

Here's an example:

What if the tire company, **Not Good Enough Year**, thought the same way. What if they thought, "Well, I know I'm supposed to make good tires and that people out there depend on me to provide them, but I'm not perfect. So, I'll just sit here and sorta throw something together and see what happens."

I imagine a lot of people driving cars and trucks will be affected by it. Some will end up in ditches and may never get to their destination. You see where I'm going with this? It's about making the effort to do the best you can. People's lives are at stake!

'Off' With The Old
And 'On' With The New

Before you were saved, you may have been in a lifestyle that you know Jesus wouldn't approve of. This could be almost anything. I won't sit here and list the many things that could fall in this category because you know the ones that pertain to you. These made up the 'old' self of your sinful nature.

Now, here's the problem. You are saved and still doing the *old* things that you used to do. Your *new* life doesn't reflect a change. You are not living by what you read in the Bible or what you are being taught at church, but by your sinful nature. It could be that you are not reading the Bible or going to church at all and are just *'winging'* your new Christian walk. It's not going to work!

This creates a bad situation in your relationship with Jesus and to others around you. You are missing out on the spiritual joy of being

saved. You are basically the 'old' you with a Jesus label. This is good if all you want is a free ticket to Eternity. But that's not what being a Christian is about. God has a purpose for you and will use you, if you let Him, to reach out to others. That's when *being saved* gets exciting and has a greater meaning in your life. Allow Him to change you!

The Suit And Tie Christian

Before I start on this topic, let me tell you that wearing a suit and tie is not a bad thing. Actually, Christians that wear suits and ties look good and I mean that. That is the main purpose of saying it: Christians that just *'look'* good. A person could be sinfully rotten to the core, but when they put a suit and tie on, they fit in with the rest of the Christians in church on Sunday morning.

Being a Christian is a spiritual thing - it's what's on the inside that counts. It's a relationship with Jesus Christ that goes straight to the heart. When this kind of relationship goes to the heart, it will begin to manifest itself outwards in our actions and in our words. Are you with me?

Many people are deceived by the *'suit and tie'* Christian because they only *'look'* good. If you were to spend some time with them, you would realize what is really going on in their heart. You could see it in their actions in the way they conduct their life. When they speak, their words coming out would make you think differently of them.

Knowing that, it is important to realize that *'walking the walk'* is more than just trying to look good. It's about *'looking good'* because of the relationship we have in Jesus and what He has placed in our heart.

Holier Than Thou Christian

I have met some Christian people that are quick to judge people. Being a Christian myself, these people were quick to tell me everything that I was doing wrong. This made me want to quit going to church and socializing with the 'Christian' people. I later learned that this type of judging is OK when you are trying to help someone and are doing it in a loving way. This should also be followed by a solution to their problem.

Pride is a killer, folks! People can easily fill themselves with the pride of being a Christian and the spiritual things they know that not only do they kill their witnessing abilities but they actually kill the chances of bringing others to Jesus. They can also kill the growth of other Christians. It's a bad deal! Jesus wasn't about all that!

If you read the Bible and learn how Jesus was, you'll learn that He never had this type of attitude toward others. He had compassion for His followers in teaching them how they should and shouldn't be and He had compassion for the ones that didn't know Him. By His example is why people chose to follow Him. He would socialize with the sinners and lead them by being the example. He didn't walk around with a stick bopping people on the hands every time they did something wrong. If He did see something wrong in a person's life, He would lovingly tell them and provide a solution. This is how we should be.

It's great to be a Christian and to have grown spiritually in our walk. But we need to understand that without God's mercy on our life and His spiritual guidance, we are nothing more than a sinner ourselves. When we meet people that are lost, we need to focus on the sin in their lives and not on that person.

And remember God loves them, too.

It's Not Just About Us
It's About Others

The day we became saved, God could have just taken us home to be with Him. We're saved! What other reason would we need to be here on Earth? Since we don't belong here anymore, we may as well just move on to Glory Land. So, why are we still here?

Listen to this:

Go ye therefore, and teach all nations, baptizing them in the name of the Father, and of the Son, and of the Holy Ghost: Teaching them to observe all things whatsoever I have commanded you: and, lo, I am with you alway, even unto the end of the world. Amen. – Matthew 28: 19, 20

Jesus said it right there. We are called to be His disciples to go out and teach others. A disciple is a follower of Jesus; to follow His teachings and to be like Him. Just like the twelve disciples in the Bible, we have a mission statement:

"To be a light in the world and to lead others to Jesus by spreading the Gospel and being an example to the world."

Being a Christian means being Christ-like. You may not know this, but being a Christian is not just about you. The world teaches us to be concerned about ourselves and nobody else. What do we want out of life? How can we make our life better? Watch television and you will discover that all of the commercial ads are directed to you.

This is not what Jesus is all about. Your Christian life should reflect the One that saved you. Why is this so important?

Here's the scenario:

- **The world is full of people that don't know Jesus as their Lord and Savior.**
- **Jesus is returning one day to take His children home.**
- **The ones that remain will burn in a lake of fire.**

Who are His children? It's the people that are saved. Does He want everyone to spend Eternity with Him? Yes, He does. Unfortunately, it's this thing called 'sin' that we talked about a few pages back that separates us. He gives us all a *'freedom of choice'*. It's a choice to turn from sin, ask for forgiveness and to turn to

Him. It's plain and simple! We have a choice!

What is our role as a Christian in all of this? The answer is to lead others to Him. It's about *'being a light in the world'*. We are the link that connects them to a relationship with Jesus. We can't save them, but we can lead them to the One that can. Is this sinking in?

This is why it's so important to truly *'walk the walk'*. It's not so that WE can live a better life, but to show others the *'better life'* we have in Jesus. Think about it!

When you start living the life Jesus wants you to have, people are going to want it, too. If they don't see a change in you, then how will they know Jesus? Time is running short! What are you waiting on? Walk the walk! Be a light!

My Testimony

A testimony is what you have after the Lord saves you or delivers you from something. It's like our story to tell others of what Jesus has done for us. Every Christian will have one. If you are saved today, you have one, too.

Our testimony is what we will use to lead others to Jesus. It is how we are able to witness to other people. Believe it or not,

that *'thing'* that Jesus delivered you from is probably what is holding a lot of people you meet back from a relationship with Jesus. It is very interesting how this works. It's like God will put people that are not saved in your life that will need to hear your testimony. The amazing thing is that they are going through the same thing or have been through it and don't know how to deal with it. All of a sudden they meet you; a person with a similar story, but this time there is a solution. His name is Jesus.

I accepted Jesus as my Lord and

Savior when I was 14 years old. My father had left me and my mother when I was five and she was forced to raise me on her own. The Lord stepped in during my teenage years because I needed a father in my life. He became my Heavenly Father!

Do you realize what happens to many teenagers growing up without a father? Let's just say that many of them end up going down the wrong roads in life. They wind up in places and situations that they shouldn't be in. God gave me His protection and put me on the path of righteousness as long as I stayed focused in it.

Within that same year, I also met Satan. I didn't really recognize him at first because he disguised himself in the things I allowed in my life. Pornography was his first trick. This is a big temptation for a young kid with raging hormones, but I took the bait. This went on for years and found its way on my computer screen as I got older.

Satan also knew I had a passion for music. I enjoyed listening to it and playing it on the guitar. Its original purpose was intended to glorify and praise God, but wound up on the stages at the local bars playing as a live band.

This introduced a new temptation given by Satan that created an addiction within me that I would later battle with in life. It's the poison called alcohol. It destroys you from the inside out and affects the people around you. Alcohol every day pushes the family away! And that's exactly what it was doing. Because of my addiction, I would be re-creating my life story all over again with my kids. They would be fatherless and the vicious cycle would continue.

That's when Jesus showed up! He woke me up when my son got saved. At that time, my son needed someone to lead him to the Lord and I wasn't able to do it. I should have been, but couldn't. My life was a mess! I had to take him to someone that could. This burned me deep and helped me realize that I needed Jesus back in my life, too. It wasn't that I need to be saved again. It was that I needed to go back to where I left Him. I had turned away.

Years later, the pornography is gone and the alcohol has been traded in for the living water that Jesus freely offers. I have been *'living'* since then. This new change has created a great life for me and my family. It has created a ministry that God has used has to reach many people and touch lives. I realize now that this was part of God's original plan before I decided to change it. I am ashamed that it took twenty years to wake me up. This is my testimony. Thank you Jesus!

Once again, the main purpose of this book is to use what the Lord has given me to share with you.

My heart goes out to all Christians everywhere – all over the world. If the lessons I have learned from my life can be used to help someone out there, then that's what I want to do. I'm sure there are Christian people out there like me that don't know what the whole deal is. Some are blinded by Satan on their purpose on this Earth and what they should be doing until the Lord comes back. I hope this book will prevent them from wasting 20 years of their life going in the wrong direction.

If you don't know Jesus as your Lord and Savior, I encourage you to make that step. Being a Christian isn't what the world says it is. It's being what Jesus wants us to be: happy and full of joy. If you need that in your life today, Jesus can and will freely give it to you. All you have to do is ask Him.

If you're a Christian, begin living by His Word and reading it daily. Don't sit around like stagnated water! Do something with the new life God has given you. Reach out to people that need this life, too. Learn more about Jesus. Live the life that He wants you to live. It brings life – life abundantly. Let's do something! You know?

I hope you received what you needed today. And please share this book with someone you know!

More From A BackPew Review

Thanks for reading this guide. We hope you enjoyed it and will continue to read our other guides in the series. Here is a complete list of our books from the series:

- **What Does It Mean To Be A Christian**
- **Acts: The Early Days Of The Christian Church**
- **Being A Dad According To The Bible**
- **The Prison Letters: Apostle Paul's Letters To The Early Church**
- **Exodus: The Journey To The Promised Land**
- **Genesis: The Beginning, The Fall And The Promise**
- **The Seven Letters: The New Testament Letters To The Early Church**
- **The Gospel From A Four-Sided View**
- **Healthy Eating: A Few Tips From The Bible**
- **Being A Man According To The Bible**
- **A Marriage Built To Last: Learn What The Bible Says About Marriage**
- **How Do I Pray? The Bible Tells Us How**
- **Revelation: The End Is Near?**